Readers Theatre in the Middle School and Junior High Classroom

A Take Part Teacher's Guide:
Springboards to Language Development
through Readers Theatre, Storytelling,
Writing, and Dramatizing!

LOIS WALKER

MERIWETHER PUBLISHING LTD.
Colorado Springs, Colorado

Meriwether Publishing Ltd., Publisher
P.O. Box 7710
Colorado Springs, CO 80933

Editor: Theodore O. Zapel
Typesetting: Susan Trinko
Cover design: Tom Myers

© Copyright MCMXCVI Take Part Productions Ltd.
Printed in the United States of America
First Edition

Library of Congress Cataloging-in-Publication Data

Walker, Lois, 1941 -
    [Readers theatre in the elementary classroom]
    Readers theatre in the middle school and junior high classroom : a take part teacher's guide : springboards to language development through readers theatre, storytelling, writing, and dramatizing! / Lois Walker.
        p.   c.m.
    Originally published: Readers theatre in the elementary classroom. North Vancouver, BC, Canada : Take Part Productions Ltd., 1990.
    Includes bibliographical references.
    ISBN 1-56608-027-4 (pbk.)
    1. Reader's theater--Study and teaching (Elementary) 2. Reader's theater--Study and teaching (Secondary) 3. Drama in education.
PN2081.R4W35   1996
371.39'9--dc21

96-43535
CIP

CONTENTS

INTRODUCTION

"Everyone needs to talk — to hear and to play with language, to exercise the mind and emotions and tongue together. Out of this spirited speech can come meaningful, flavorful language, worth the time and effort of writing and rewriting, phrasing, rehearsing, and reading aloud."

(Source: Wolsch, R.A. and Wolsch, L.A.C. *From Speaking to Writing to Reading: Relating the Arts of Communication.* New York, Columbia University Teachers College. Used to introduce SECTION 6: Sharing Stories, Poems and Songs. *Enhancing and Evaluating Oral Communication in the Primary Grades.* Student Assessment Branch, Ministry of Education, Province of British Columbia, Canada, January, 1988.)

WHAT IS READERS THEATRE?

THE CONCEPT GROWS

If you hadn't come in contact with the term Readers Theatre until now, it was probably only a matter of time! The concept of preparing scripts for reading rather than memorizing and acting is not new, but is a growing practice which has spawned a variety of learned publications, university courses, Script Services in the United States and Canada, a yearly international Readers Theatre Summer Institute and more. As a teaching strategy, Readers Theatre procedures have been examined and publicized through publications of the International Reading Association and the Australian Reading Association among others. The list continues to grow.

ORAL INTERPRETATION

So, what is Readers Theatre? It is literature-based oral reading which communicates story through oral interpretation. In its most simple form, Readers Theatre is hardly theatre at all! As in theatre, a script is used, but the story information is communicated by readers who take on narrator and character parts. Lines are read rather than memorized. The story is read by readers who stand or sit in fixed positions and address their lines directly to a listening audience.

A DRAMATIC APPROACH TO LITERATURE

According to the late Mel White, author of the "Readers Theatre Anthology," Readers Theatre is simply "a dramatic approach to literature." Not only are published play scripts read by Readers Theatre enthusiasts, "but all types of literature: short stories, novels, poems, letters, essays, diaries, radio and television scripts, and news columns. This interpretive art form is so varied in presentation that is has numerous names: Interpreters Theatre, Chamber Theatre, Platform Theatre, Concert Reading, Group Reading, Multiple Reading, Staged Reading, Theatre of the Mind, and Drama of the Living Voice. Suffice it to say, it is called Readers Theatre by most, a medium in which two or more oral interpreters through their oral reading, with their bodies and voices, cause an audience to experience literature as they, the interpreters, experience it. Some have called this 'putting the human being back into the literature, physically, vocally, intellectually, and emotionally.'"

CREATIVE ORAL READING

Readers Theatre, then, is creative oral reading of any type of literature which can be orally interpreted in a dramatic way. Mel White suggests, "this means it has characters speaking in order to express their thoughts, viewpoints, and emotions. It has characters interacting with other characters, with situations, or even in conflict with their own inner thoughts. In Readers Theatre, two or more readers use their voices and bodies to reveal the actions and attitudes of the characters created by an author, be that author a playwright, novelist, short story writer, essayist, news columnist or poet. It calls for mental images of characters playing out a scene that exists primarily in the minds of the participants - and these participants are both the readers and the listeners." It is sometimes oral reading, it sometimes comes close to conventional theatre, but no matter the final approach, Readers Theatre requires more use of the imagination from both readers and listeners than any other theatre form.

READERS THEATRE AS PERFORMANCE

If you are a drama teacher, and performance is your Readers Theatre goal, you and your students have much work ahead of you. A successful Readers Theatre performance takes as much rehearsal time as a play. If you are performance orientated, Mel White warns, Readers Theatre "is not an exercise in sight reading. It is not an under-rehearsed performance of some piece of literature with a cast of readers with their noses buried in their scripts because they are unfamiliar with them." A Readers Theatre production often takes more rehearsal time than a play because the interpreters do not have the assistance of "those theatrical embellishments": sets, props, wigs, makeup, special costuming, lights, etc. Without these embellishments to aid communication, Readers Theatre readers must do it all! They must make the literature come alive using only their voices, gestures, facial expressions, and dramatic stage presence. Also, we are not talking about a "script-in-hand walk through of a staged play, looking like a dress rehearsal that did not get its lines learned." Readers Theatre will become a whole new kind of challenge for your drama students!

READERS THEATRE AS A TEACHING STRATEGY

The idea that Readers Theatre might serve as a teaching tool, without ever taking students to a "staged performance level" is still a growing concept. What an idea! Over the past few years I've met and worked with a number of incredible teachers who are not trained drama teachers, not performance oriented, but have found Readers Theatre to be a great teaching technique! Many of these teachers have been involved with Special Education: Inclusion or Mainstreaming, and ESL (English Second Language) teachers who are trying to teach young people who are learning English as a second language. In the regular classroom, Readers Theatre just makes reading FUN! Talk about Whole Language! Talk about strategies that work!

With the right scripts and the right attitude, reluctant readers and ESL students thrive in a Readers Theatre situation. Teachers tell me that self-confidence, self-esteem, oral reading skills, presentation skills, cooperative group skills, and vocabulary skills blossomed when they utilized Readers Theatre scripts in their classrooms. Students in regular classrooms benefited from all of the above and simply enjoyed the whole experience by exhibiting a growing love of literature! I'm not surprised. What could be more fun than taking part in the oral reading of a great story? What could be more fun than getting the chance to be "a bit of an actor" without the terrible stress of being onstage (especially if you're not quite ready for that experience)? What better way to encourage a love of reading than to introduce Readers Theatre for the stressless fun and experience of all?

In an article for the Australian Reading Association, titled "Reading and Writing Readers Theatre Scripts," Charlene C. Swanson compares Readers Theatre with drama as tools for teaching in the classroom. She says that "both drama and Readers Theatre provide students with rich learning opportunities. Yet many teachers (except possibly Drama or English teachers) shy away from involving students in dramatic performances because certain aspects of a dramatic performance appear to be overwhelming obstacles: directing, costuming, blocking, set design, props, makeup and rehearsal time. Even when teachers feel competent to handle these details, the reality of the increased workload involved in producing a play may be enough to reduce their efforts to one performance a year. But Readers Theatre is much easier to implement."

READERS THEATRE STRATEGIES

IMPLEMENTATION

Readers Theatre is so new that some of its forms are still emerging. Ways to implement Readers Theatre in the classroom range from in-class Circle Reading, Instant Reading, Cooperative Reading, or Staged Reading experiences to the more sophisticated performance-oriented Chamber Theatre and Story Theatre approaches. For middle school and junior high classroom purposes, Circle Reading, Instant Reading, Cooperative Reading, and Staged Reading are the most useful and effective in-class strategies. Following are procedural descriptions of these four methods.

CIRCLE READINGS

Circle Readings allow readers to read all the different parts, experiment with voices, and, eventually, choose favorite roles. This method helps build reader confidence because it is nonthreatening, noncompetitive, and gives all readers a chance to read all roles.

EIGHT STEPS TO A SUCCESSFUL CIRCLE READING

Step 1: Duplicate classroom scripts for your readers. (To get you started, two classroom scripts are included at the back of this guide, starting on page 31.)

Step 2: Ask your readers to silently read through the entire story.

Step 3: After all readers have read the story silently, gather readers into a large circle. Include yourself in the circle, if possible.

Step 4: Next, begin by asking the reader on your left to read the first reader's part in the script, the next person to read the second reader's part, and so on. No individual reading parts are assigned at this point. Each reader reads in turn around the circle. The teacher can, and probably should, join in on the reading too.

Step 5: When the circle has completed the story, take time to discuss readers' parts. What does each character look like? What kind of personalities do they have? How might they sound? How would each character stand or sit? What might each character wear?

Step 6: Discuss the importance of each narrator. Explore how the narrators introduce the story, fill in all the narrative details, set the proper mood for the story action, and help the character readers

5

set and keep the right reading pace.

Step 7: Review meanings and pronunciations of any difficult words.

Step 8: Now, ask your readers to volunteer for specific reading parts. Ask each volunteer to underline his or her lines, then read the script aloud again. Swap parts and scripts around the circle and read again. Continue until interest lags or time runs out.

INSTANT READINGS

Instant Readings are perfect rainy day activities, or a great way to fill in a few minutes during or at the end of a day. A script may be read once or twice, put away, then reintroduced throughout the school year. By following the steps below, a teacher can immediately involve students in a meaningful reading activity.

EIGHT STEPS TO A SUCCESSFUL INSTANT READING

Step 1: Duplicate classroom scripts, as needed.

Step 2: Pass scripts to all class members, or ask students to share scripts in pairs.

Step 3: Ask students to read through the scripts silently.

Step 4: Assign parts to various members of the class. Ask them to take a few minutes to underline or highlight their assigned lines in the script. Ask readers to write their character name or reader number on the front of the script.

Step 5: Now assigned readers can read the story aloud from their seats. Correct pronunciations, clarify meanings, and ask readers to make notes on their scripts, if needed. Try to keep the reading moving, however!

Step 6: Next, ask the same readers to assemble in front of class for the second reading.

Step 7: When this reading is completed, discuss (story, reading, or both), reassess parts, swap scripts, and read again.

Step 8: Continue until interest lags. Collect scripts. You might want to have a classroom reading of this type on a regular basis, once or twice a week.

COOPERATIVE READING

If you are planning to involve your entire class in Cooperative Reading groups, simply duplicate scripts with appropriate numbers of readers. (Many Readers Theatre scripts feature five to eight readers. Five scripts needing five readers will equally divide a class of twenty five, etc.)

SIX STEPS TO SUCCESSFUL COOPERATIVE READINGS

Step 1: Assemble students into groups. Pass out scripts.

Step 2: Ask students to read through their scripts silently. Then assign practice spaces to each group. Groups may now break away and go to their practice spaces.

Step 3: Using cooperative learning techniques, each group assigns parts and rehearses its script. Suggestions for improvements, additions or changes must come from the group. The teacher may move from group to group encouraging the readers. Check to see that scripts have been underlined, as previously mentioned.

Step 4: Ask readers to take scripts home so that some home rehearsal may be accomplished. Suggest reading the script aloud with various family members.

Step 5: Allow groups to practice two or three times, or until they feel ready for an audience.

Step 6: Schedule the group presentations. You might feature one group presentation per day for a week, or hold a "Friday Festival" and present them all on the following Friday afternoon.

NOTE: You need not include all class members in a Cooperative Reading presentation. Selected groups may rehearse scripts for presentations at different times throughout the school year.

REHEARSING THE INSTANT AND COOPERATIVE READINGS

Charlene C. Swanson suggests the following rehearsal plan when using an Instant, Cooperative, or Circle reading approach. It is an eight-point procedure which enables any teacher to get the most from student readers. She says:

"The rehearsal is the essence of Readers Theatre. Here is where students get practice becoming fluent oral readers. They must understand the story before they can use their voices to convey that interpretation to others.

Repeated readings in a Readers Theatre setting is not tedious, but fun."

The eight point procedure:

1. First, students read the script silently to get the main idea. Younger students can read it aloud with the teacher or listen to an older group of children performing the script. They might follow along with their fingers while they listen.

2. Then, assign the parts to individual students. Be sure that longer, more difficult parts do not go to the poorer or less confident readers for the first few readings of a script.

3. When using a script for the first time, have students find and underline the name of their part each time it appears in the left margin of the script. Then have them write that character's name on the front of the script. As students change parts, they exchange scripts.

4. Students then rehearse their parts and ask each other or the teacher for help with unknown words.

5. Now read the script aloud. Remind students to say the line the way that the character would say it and to follow any voice directions included by the script writer. Also, remind them to follow along when others are reading so they will be ready to read when their turn arrives.

6. After the first reading, discuss the story as a group. Focus on how each character feels in this situation. Explore some different ways a reader might communicate feeling through voice.

7. Now have the students do a second oral reading, keeping the same parts.

8. Use of a particular script with a particular group of students can end at this point, but some groups will not be ready to stop. One option is to switch parts. This is a good time for the less able readers to read a larger part. The swapping of parts may take place over several days. Stop each day's lesson before students become bored. Time limits will vary with age and script.

ADDITIONAL STRATEGIES

A teacher's approach to the reading experience will vary with the ages of the readers, their reading levels, and the difficulty of the script. Here are some additional strategies a teacher might try:

* Encourage class members to research the tale in depth. Is it a folk or fairy tale, myth or legend? In what country was the story originally told? Has the story motif been identified in other countries too? If so, what special form did the story take? Are there similarities and/or differences?

* Discuss the story with readers by examining the individual characters, type of story, and story themes. Is the story worth rehearsing and sharing? Why? Why not?

* Encourage readers to speak their lines the way their character would say the lines. Experiment with theatricalized voices.

* Discuss with readers how each character feels as the story progresses. Suggest some different ways the readers can show the characters' inner feelings through their voices, facial expressions, and posture.

* Suggest that readers write notes upon their own scripts. Readers might underline important words to be stressed, mark pauses and inflections, or indicate good places for taking a needed breath. Other performance tips may be written in the margin.

* Encourage all readers and listeners to help "direct" the reading by commenting, critiquing, adding suggestions.

* Stress oral clarity. Is the reader reading too fast, or too slowly? Does the reader need to concentrate on enunciation, articulation, or pronunciation of certain words? Can the reader be heard by *all* listeners?

* Suggest the addition of costume pieces or props, if desired. It's important to remember, however, that Readers Theatre scripts don't really require any theatricalized effects. They need only to be read aloud with expression, enthusiasm, and enjoyment! These scripts have been written and designed to make oral reading *fun*.

Remember that much of your instructional task will be automatically transferred to your students. According to Dr. William Adams, Director of the Institute for Readers Theatre:

"The student becomes engrossed with the fun of 'giving a play' and the oblique learning follows naturally from this self-motivating force. The student is aware of the pleasures of the activity, and only the teacher is aware of the many skills being taught ... Students have a natural curiosity and ability to create. Somewhere in the educational process, unfortunately, these innate talents are often stifled, and the students begin to restrict their imaginations. Readers Theatre is an effective device which can be used to restore young people's rightful progression to image and create."

FOUR SPECIALIZED IN-CLASS APPLICATIONS FOR READERS THEATRE SCRIPTS

COOPERATIVE LEARNING

Divide the class into groups. Distribute scripts to each member in the group. Ask each group to work together to prepare the script readings for oral presentation. Group members will be responsible for assigning parts, preparing a rehearsal schedule, rehearsing, selecting, designing, and creating stage props or costume pieces (if needed), and encouraging effective, fluent, expressive oral readings. Stage movement may be taken directly from the suggestions in the teacher's script which accompanies each Take Part Read-Aloud Story Script, or, alternatively, may be devised by the group itself. Encourage group members to contribute their own ideas and to express support for the ideas of other group members. All group members should be encouraged to participate.

For true cooperation to take place, each member must realize that *all* readers are needed to produce a polished, successful presentation. No *one* reader can carry the performance. Any individual effort is just *one part* of the finished product. As in any traditional "theatre" project, *all* actors must work together toward a successful "opening night!"

After the readings have been presented, ask all group members to think back over the experience, identify the problems which arose during rehearsal and performance, and write them down. Then ask group members to record everything the group did to solve the problems. Ask group members to list what they would do differently the next time they prepare a reader script for performance, focusing only on *constructive*, not *negative* behaviors. Give the students ten minutes to discuss this information within their groups, then ask each group to report to the rest of the class the behaviors which worked for it.

SPECIAL ED. AND ENGLISH AS A SECOND LANGUAGE (ESL)

Students who speak little English or are reading at a lower level than their peers especially enjoy the reader scripts which feature a simple yet interesting plot, rhyming or chanting, and extensive use of repetitive words and phrases. These students are generally happy to join in on the simpler lines, phrases, and sentences, while a more accomplished student reader (or the teacher) takes the more difficult lines, or acts as the major narrator. This particular procedure also works with *special* students who join a regular classroom for specific course study. When the *special* teacher knows students' reading levels, knows the scripts well, and helps choose reading parts carefully, *special* students can successfully join in on a Readers Theatre reading in the regular classroom. Middle school and junior high special and ESL students often enjoy rehearsing primary level scripts and then performing the story for younger children within the school system or at the local library. This procedure may also be used by continuing education and ESL adult readers who rehearse together to prepare a simple story which will be performed for younger listeners. The opportunities are endless!

Rehearsal is the key! As *special* and *ESL* students rehearse a script over and over again, strange words become familiar, confidence is built, and readers start to feel more comfortable with the language. As in most theatre experiences, participants develop a "team spirit" through rehearsal which helps them feel part of a larger "whole," working together toward a final goal. In Readers Theatre, no one feels alone. This is important to *all* readers, but is especially important to special and ESL readers who may already feel quite "alone."

Because the special and ESL student assumes the role of a character in the reader script, a contextual framework is established for reading out (speaking) the part. This allows the student to experience dialog, not memorize a list. This context assists with learning the connotative, as well as, denotative meanings of words.

SPEECH THERAPY STUDENTS AND SPECIAL STUDENT MAINSTREAMING

Special students and students involved in speech therapy may feel apprehensive when included or mainstreamed into the regular classroom. Having the students take a part in a Readers Theatre experience is one way to involve the students in either a small or large classroom group immediately. Depending upon a student's abilities, he or she may take a reading part and quickly become an important member of a classroom reading performance. As part of a group which is working closely together, the *special* student takes a giant step toward integration.

Like all people, students with special needs enjoy make-believe, play-acting, and group activities. Even watching and listening to "a play" being performed or read is fun. Do not underestimate what this type of enthusiasm and interest can do to enhance learning. A student with speech language problems may find Readers Theatre a comfortable way to listen to and practice speech patterns and sound/symbol relationships.

BUDDY READING

Readers Theatre scripts may be read aloud by two or three readers simply by doubling up on parts. If your school participates in Buddy Reading activities with a local elementary school, Readers Theatre scripts can be valuable resources. When reading from a Readers Theatre script, simply assign the appropriate reading part (or parts) to the reluctant reader. The older "buddy" reader reads all the other parts. As the story is read over and over again, your reluctant reader will become so familiar with the text that he or she may ask to take over more of the reading! Don't forget that "buddy readers" may also wish to rehearse and then perform for the class or other "buddy" pairs.

CASTING, STAGING, AND PERFORMING THE READINGS

Staged Readings require a rehearsed, polished, and more stylized Readers Theatre performance. Readers are assigned positions in a designated "stage" area, entrances and exits are planned and rehearsed, and close attention is paid to gestures, facial expressions, simple costume pieces, and other performance aspects of the chosen script. The two scripts found at the back of this guide include special "teacher versions" which suggest possible stage set-ups, entrance and exit techniques, and other important directorial information which you may want to use when planning a Staged Reading.

STAGED READING TRY-OUTS: Five Teacher Guidelines

GUIDELINE 1: Make scripts available to all readers who are interested in taking part in the Staged Reading. The scripts may be taken home for practice before try-out day.

GUIDELINE 2: On tryout day, assemble readers as you would for a Circle Reading as described in the Circle Reading section of this guide. To warm up your readers, simply ask your readers to read the script around the circle in a fun, nonthreatening way.

GUIDELINE 3: When the group is warmed up, assign specific parts to specific readers and read through the script again. Encourage all readers to volunteer for the parts they like best, paying close attention to any shy or reluctant readers in the group. Read the script through over and over again until all readers are satisfied.

GUIDELINE 4: If possible, cast the Staged Reading as you sit there in the circle. Ask the readers to help you choose the cast. If *fun* is your goal, why not let each reader choose his or her own favorite part? If this approach is not possible, *you* will make the decision. Announce the casting and also post a cast list somewhere in the room.

GUIDELINE 5: You will also need to post a rehearsal schedule to let your cast know when and where practices will be held, how much time will be required, and the date, time, and place of the actual performance.

STAGED READING REHEARSALS: Twelve Teacher Guidelines

GUIDELINE 1: At the first rehearsal, make sure each reader has a script. Ask your readers to write their character names *and* their real names on the front of their scripts. Next, ask cast members to highlight or underline their own lines. Provide colorful highlighters, pens, or pencils, for this job.

GUIDELINE 2: Once highlighting is done, seat readers in a circle and ask them to read the script aloud. Many scripts feature special sections where all readers read in unison, together (a choral reading approach). Pay special attention to these sections, rehearsing the readers until they develop a feel for the proper rhythm and flow of the words or phrases.

GUIDELINE 3: From the very beginning, suggest improvements to a reader's projection, posture, pronunciation, intonation, facial expressions, etc., by referring to the *character* rather than the actual reader. To soften criticism, try saying, "Witch, use your loudest cackle and scariest voice on that line," rather than, "Janice, I can't hear a word you are saying!"

GUIDELINE 4: As rehearsals progress, try to practice in the actual room where you will be giving your performance. If this is impossible, mark off an area which is similar to the stage or performance space you will using on performance day. Arrange your readers, seated, standing, or both, in that space and continue to work on interpretations.

GUIDELINE 5: When directing, always use proper stage directions. STAGE RIGHT and LEFT are your *readers'* right or left, not yours as you stand facing the readers. UPSTAGE is behind your readers. DOWNSTAGE is in front of your readers, just in front of the audience:

UPSTAGE

STAGE RIGHT　　　　　　　　**(Readers)**　　　　　　　　**STAGE LEFT**

DOWNSTAGE

++

AUDIENCE

GUIDELINE 6: Rehearse entrances, exits, and any stage movements until they run smoothly and readers feel comfortable with them. More specific information about entrances can be found on page 15 of this guide.

GUIDELINE 7: You will probably find that *lack of vocal projection* will be your biggest rehearsal problem. Encourage your readers to *project, shout, yell!* If your readers speak too quickly or too slowly, remind them to practice at home, concentrate on the specific problem, and go over their lines so often that they become very familiar with them. This type of familiarity usually makes for a well-paced performance in the end.

GUIDELINE 8: All through the rehearsal process, ask for the opinions of your cast members. Be open to creative suggestions about practice and presentation. Try out new ideas and ask cast members to help decide what works and what does not.

GUIDELINE 9: If costume pieces, props, sound effects, or special signs have been added to the presentation, have at least two full dress rehearsals (including all additions) just prior to the performance date. Iron out any extra problems these additions cause during these rehearsals.

GUIDELINE 10: Stress oral interpretation. Rehearse until the piece runs smoothly, but don't ask readers to memorize lines. This is still a *readers* presentation.

GUIDELINE 11: If possible, hold one last full dress rehearsal in front of an audience. Perhaps another class or the principal and office staff will act as the audience. It is always a good idea to work in front of a live audience at least once before the actual performance.

GUIDELINE 12: On performance day, be positive! Readers Theatre is fun. If the cast enjoys themselves, so will the audience. It's guaranteed!

POLISHING THE READING

During rehearsals, the director should encourage readers to explore each character part in depth. Emphasizing eye contact, diction, character development, controlled movement or mime, and performance energy will help achieve a well-paced, well-rehearsed performance.

When appropriate, help readers examine the feelings of each character. How does a character feel at the beginning of the tale? How and why do those feelings change as the story progresses? In what ways might each reader communicate these feelings to the listeners? Encourage the use of vocal and volume changes, facial expressions, posture, and varying tempo patterns.

Encourage readers to use their imaginations by adding more elements to the reading performance, if desired. Special hats or costume pieces, masks, props or signs can often help readers tell the tale in a more theatricalized fashion. Keep the additions simple, remembering that some readers will be required to hold the script folder in one hand while managing a prop in the other.

STAGED READING ENTRANCES

Readers Theatre scripts may include suggested entrance directions for all cast readers. Usually the direction from which a cast member enters will not matter as readers may enter from any off-stage areas. Don't be concerned if no off-stage areas are available to your performing space. It is possible to have readers enter from the back of the room, walking through or around the audience.

Of course, formal entrances are not necessary, but they *do* have a place in polished staged reading performances. If done correctly, staged entrances help the audience identify certain important characters, and set the mood and tone for the entire reading.

Here is a simple entrance which might be used for any Readers Theatre script reading:

Arrange readers off-stage as they are listed, in order, at the front of your script. Each cast member will carry his or her script in the upstage hand (furthest from the audience).

On a given signal, all cast members walk into the performance space, line up in a semicircle, and face the audience. On another signal, readers lift their script folders to chest height and open scripts to the first page.

At this point, you may wish to have each reader introduce him or herself. One by one each reader steps forward: "My name is Janice Cook and I am reading the part of Helen in The Trojan Horse." Each reader steps back into line when finished. After the last introduction, the reading begins.

Ask your cast members to speak directly to the audience, not to each other. (There may be some *special* times when you will break this rule and ask characters on stage to look at and react to each other.) Generally, however, cast members will focus upon the audience just as a storyteller focuses upon the listeners. It is sometimes helpful for cast members to focus eyes slightly above the heads of audience members.

SCRIPT FOLDERS

If possible, place cast scripts in colorful folders. Ring binders allow for smooth and easy page turning. If ring binders are not available, staple cast scripts along left hand side into simple cardboard folders. Crease the pages about a half an inch inside the staples for easy page turning. Never staple in upper left or right corner.

Some readers may prefer to read from loose pages arranged in sequence in a folder. Loose pages are the easiest to turn over but must be kept in order.

Remind readers to hold script folders down and away from their bodies. Readers may need to experiment to find comfortable and workable positions. Explain that facial expressions must be seen by the listeners, and spoken words must not be muffled by folders.

EDUCATIONAL VALUES OF READERS THEATRE REHEARSAL

Whether you choose a simple instant reading approach or a polished staged reading, remember that your readers will get more from the scripted experience if they are encouraged to "rehearse" by reading the stories repeatedly. Words and phrases which might be beyond a reader's demonstrated reading level can, through repetition, be more easily assimilated into a working vocabulary. Words are absorbed through repetitive drill, but done so without a tedious list of unrelated drill words. Instead, "drill" becomes "rehearsal" for the telling of a story, a play of words, a theatrical experience.

USING READERS THEATRE AS A SPRINGBOARD TO LANGUAGE DEVELOPMENT

SPRINGBOARDS TO STORYTELLING: TWELVE STORYTELLING ACTIVITIES

"Storytelling can be an all-encompassing learning activity. The study of mythology, folktales and fairy lore can in turn lead to the study of history, geography and traditions. The background information available in the research of a good story is intriguing and never ending. The knowledge one gains simply from organizing the materials and learning research techniques is valuable in all other study areas. The skills that are gained in public speaking will be valuable for a lifetime."

From "Students as Storytellers" by Barbara Budge Griffin from her "Guidebook Storyteller Series." 1989, 10 South Keeneway Drive, Medford, OR 97504, USA.

Once a Readers Theatre script has been introduced to, and used with your class for some time, you may wish to springboard the script reading experience into a variety of *storytelling* projects and activities. At this point in the process, your students will be well acquainted with the narrative line of the story and be ready to move from *reading* to *telling*.

Activity 1: Remembering and Repeating the Story.

After reading a Readers Theatre script, discuss the story with your class. Be certain to identify and examine the story's *main idea*. Outline the story's sequence of action by charting it on the board. Ask chosen students to retell parts or all of the story. You might divide the class into small cooperative groups and continue the retellings in this manner.

Activity 2: Story Webbing or Clustering.

A good way to remember a story is to write, in *any* order, the key words or brief phrases of the story, then connect them in proper sequence.

Ask your students to take out a sheet of paper and draw circles upon the paper. Each circle represents a remembered part of the story. Students may draw their circles at random or in a clockwise pattern.

Now, ask students to write brief descriptions (or draw remembered story parts) inside these circles using one idea per circle. Important: students may use only the space inside the circles. This restriction limits random thought and encourages students to be concise.

Last, tell students to number each circle in the order of its occurrence in

21

the story and join the circles by drawing lines from one circle to another (Circle 1 is joined to Circle 2, Circle 3 is joined to Circle 4, etc.)

Activity 3: Storyboarding

All students enjoy storyboarding because it is just like drawing a comic strip. Movie directors storyboard their scripts so that they are able to visualize how the action will look when it is filmed by the camera. The storyboard is a drawn representation of the story in which each drawing represents a major scene or action. The drawings can be done with stick figures and in comic book fashion, but no words are used.

Ask students to take out a large sheet of paper, draw a series of large squares on the paper, and fill in these squares with their storyboard drawings. Don't forget to write the name of the story and the artist's name at the top. The exercise is meant to help students organize ideas through an understandable format and encourage proper selection and organization of details used to develop a plot.

Activity 4: Story Mapping

For another sequencing and remembering activity, ask students to prepare a story map of the script story. On a large sheet of paper, students may sketch all locations mentioned in the story. These might include mountains, villages, rivers, lakes, the tennis courts, a character's home, an inn, the graveyard, etc.

Now ask students to connect these locations with lines which are just like the lines on a map. The map is meant to start at the beginning of the story and lead us through the story, sequence by sequence, from start to finish. The map makers will draw the path of the story's action. Display these colorful maps around the classroom.

Activity 5: Determining Story Type

After reading a script, identify the story type. Consider the following classifications:

FABLE	A story told to teach a lesson. The tale often involves talking animals.
FAIRY TALE	The characters in a fairy tale are capable of magical deeds. Some of these characters will be human, some will not.
FOLKTALE	A story which was told by and handed down from the

common people.

MYTH   A story which attempts to explain the customs of a group or a phenomenon of nature.

LEGEND   A story which is believed to have a historical basis, occurred in the past, and has been handed down through generations.

Activity 6: Videotaping the Tellers

After reading a script, discussing it in class, and doing some sequencing, suggest that students retell the story (or favorite parts of the story) in their own words. Rehearsal may be accomplished cooperatively in small groups or individually. The tellings will be prepared for classroom videotaping.

Because video is a visual medium, encourage tellers to retell the story in a variety of ways. Costumes, puppets, masks, drawings, props, hats, or signs may add just the visual variety needed for this type of project. Important: all retellings must be kept to a specified time limit. The limit will probably be determined by tellers' ages, number of tellers, length of tape cassette, availability of video equipment, etc.

If time permits, tape the tellings, play them back, discuss the performances, and tape the tellings again. When tellers are happy with their renditions, save and store the tape. At a later date, invite parents, your principal, or another class in for a staged reading performance of the story and a taped showing of the retellings.

Activity 7: Researching Variant Stories

Many Readers Theatre scripts are adapted from well-known folktales, fairy tales, myths, or legends. Send students to the library in search of parallel or variant versions of the scripted tale. Ask students to read variant versions aloud to the class.

Divide the class into as many groups as you have variant versions. Assign one variant story version to each group. Each group will retell its assigned story to the whole class, using any method it deems fit. (Circle or tandem-telling, dramatization, mime, puppet or mask presentation, etc.)

After performances, ask students which versions they preferred, and why.

Activity 8: Summarizing a Story

A story summary attempts to provide an overview of the story. This can be written in paragraph form, including names and descriptions of the main characters, and a statement which summarizes all important story points.

In writing a story summary consider the who, what, when, where and how of the plot. For example, *who* was involved in the story, *what* was the problem, *when* did it happen, *where* did the action take place, *how* was the problem solved?

As budding storytellers, your students will also want to include in their summaries the first and last sentences of the story, and any key phrases, poems, chants, or sentences which need to be memorized. These summaries will come in handy when storytellers begin to rehearse their stories, putting the plot into their own words.

Activity 9: Studying the Characters

After they have read the script, ask your students to study the characters involved in the plot. Well-prepared storytellers know their characters so well that they can actually "see" each character through their imaginations. Ask students to prepare a written description of each character in the story.

Here are some character considerations: height, shape, weight, prominent features, clothing. Personality traits are important, so envision ways of speaking, ways of moving, and any other revealing mannerisms. Determine hair color, eye color, voice quality, ethnic origins. Examine each character's temperament, moods, and mood changes within the story. Describe the relationship of each character to other characters in the story.

Remember, storytellers will not necessarily tell about these character descriptions when retelling the story. This exercise is meant to help each teller become so familiar with the characters that the story becomes "real" and *belongs* to the teller. Method actors consider characters in much the same way when preparing for a role.

Activity 10: Sequencing

When preparing a story for telling, it is important to go over the *sequence of events* as often as possible. Encourage your storytellers to do this mentally, and also to write the sequence (the order of the story's action) in list form.

Tellers will benefit from dividing the story into its major sections, then describing those sections with a few key words. Ask students to number down the left hand side of a piece of paper. They will need as many numbers as there are story parts or sections. Students may then describe each story part beside a number, working down the page until story's end.

Most budding tellers will want to memorize this numbered sequence list, because it provides them with the framework and basic structure of the story. Once the framework is in place, each teller can add a "personal flavor" by describing the details in his or her own words.

Activity 11: Retelling the Story in the Teller's Own Words

After the reading of a script, divide your class into small cooperative groups and encourage each group to prepare a *retelling* of the same story in "their own words." (This project can also be assigned to individuals, rather than groups.) It is important to remember that a story script, meant to be read aloud, may need some changing and restructuring if it is now to be *told* rather than *read*.

Encourage students to use the story plot, but turn it into a more tellable tale by:

(a) creating an attention-getting beginning.

(b) cutting minor characters from the story, if they seem to confuse the telling.

(c) concentrating on one main storyline which is clear, complete and easy to follow.

(d) emphasizing the *action* of the story.

(e) building the action so that it steadily moves toward a suitable climax.

(f) working to and creating a satisfying conclusion.

(g) creating a solid and concise final sentence on which to end the tale.

NOTE: Tellers may want to return to their reader script and *memorize* any phrases which are repeated throughout the tale, poems, chants, or rhymes, suitable beginning and ending sentences, or specially worded bits of dialog. Otherwise, the story should be retold in their own words.

Activity 12: Evaluating the Readings and Retellings

There are many evaluation forms available to teachers of public speaking, acting, storytelling, and oral reading. Evaluation suggests attention to the following:

* Pronunciation and enunciation. Can the speaker's words be heard and understood? Are the words pronounced clearly and smoothly?

* Eye contact. Is eye contact with the audience or fellow actors utilized properly and maintained?

* Timing or pacing. Is the story told at a comfortable pace, or is the telling too fast, too slow, or lacking in variety?

* Story familiarity. Do the tellers know the story well? Did the tellers remember the proper sequence, put the story into their own words, memorize needed phrases or poems, and tell the story smoothly from beginning to end?

* Gestures. Did the tellers use gestures which seemed spontaneous and relaxed? Were the tellers poised and confident?

* Voice control. Did tellers use their voices to help create characters, add variety in pitch and volume, create the proper mood, or aid in a build-up to the story's climax?

* Story suitability. Was the story a suitable one for the age and experience of the tellers, for the audience, and for the occasion?

* Overview. How would you evaluate the overall presentation? Did the telling work?

SPRINGBOARDS TO WRITING: TWENTY-SIX WRITING ACTIVITIES

"Writing seems to us to be one of the most important ways to assure that all students master the basic literacy skills and allow them freedom to express their own concerns and build upon their special interests. In fact, over several years of work with middle and junior high students, we have become convinced that full development of literacy skills can occur only when these students do a lot of writing as well as a lot of reading. Further, we have learned that young people write a lot only when they are encouraged and expected to write about things they want to write about. ...We find that activities which encourage students to communicate their own ideas, discoveries, and feelings, particularly in written form, are a way of promoting rigorous learning."

"Children's Writing," Leonard Sealey, Nancy Sealey, and Marcia Millmore. International Reading Association. 1979. Newark, DE, 19711, USA.

Once a Readers Theatre script has been introduced to your class through repeated instant readings or staged readings, you may wish to springboard these experiences into a variety of *writing* projects and activities. At this point in the process, your students will be well acquainted with the storyline, and ready to move from *reading* the story to *writing about* the story in a number of creative ways.

ACTIVITY 1.　Rewrite the story from the point of view of any one of the major or minor characters.

ACTIVITY 2.　Write a television commercial advertising the fun of Readers Theatre. Try to encourage other classes to "buy" the Readers Theatre experience.

ACTIVITY 3.　Write an imaginary autobiography of one of the main or minor characters found in the story.

ACTIVITY 4.　Compile an imaginary diary as it might have been written by one of the main or minor characters found in the story.

ACTIVITY 5.　Write an original poem which retells the scripted story or summarizes the plot.

ACTIVITY 6.　Rewrite the script as a play and stage it for another class, an assembly program, or a gathering of parents.

ACTIVITY 7.　Write a puppet play based on the story from the script. Make puppets, rehearse, and perform for a young audience.

ACTIVITY 8.　Write a new ending to the story found in your script.

ACTIVITY 9.　Write a newspaper article about the story, or an episode in the story, found in the Readers Theatre script. Try a new approach. Write it as a feature story. Could it work as an advice column? How about a cooking column?

ACTIVITY 10.　Write a letter of recommendation for one of your favorite Readers Theatre scripts.

ACTIVITY 11.　Write an imaginary letter from one character in a Readers Theatre script to another.

ACTIVITY 12.　Create funny newspaper headlines and apply them to the characters found in one of your favorite Readers Theatre scripts.

ACTIVITY 13.　Rewrite a Readers Theatre script as a radio play with sound effects and music.

ACTIVITY 14.　Create an alphabet book with each letter representing a character or situation found in a script.

ACTIVITY 15. Develop a series of crossword puzzles based on a script's characters, locations, plot development and action.

ACTIVITY 16. Write a newspaper advertisement for your favorite Readers Theatre script.

ACTIVITY 17. Rewrite the story found in a Readers Theatre script as a modern soap opera seen on TV.

ACTIVITY 18. Write a personality sketch of one of the characters found in your favorite Readers Theatre script.

ACTIVITY 19. Compose a folk song about a story's character or an event in the story. You might write the song around a common chorus which describes the essence of the tale.

ACTIVITY 20. Rewrite the story in a Readers Theatre script into a story which is designed to be *read aloud* to younger children.

ACTIVITY 21. Rewrite the story in a Readers Theatre script into an *illustrated* book for younger children.

ACTIVITY 22. Rewrite a Readers Theatre script as a *musical* play destined for Broadway! Rehearse and perform.

ACTIVITY 23. Write limericks which relate to the story found in a Readers Theatre script. A limerick is a humorous, five-line poem which has a rhyme scheme of A-A-B-B-A. Lines 1, 2 and 5 rhyme with each other and lines 3 and 4 also rhyme with each other. Here are two examples from a Take Part Read-Aloud Story Script, "Big Brother and the Elfin Woman."

> A youth met a talkative elf,
> Who only gave thought to herself.
> She talked, whined, and lied,
> Until the youth cried,
> "I wish you'd stayed trapped on the shelf!"

> A sports fan who lived in the cold,
> Met an Elfin, obnoxious and bold.
> The elf had a brother,
> Unlike any other,
> Who taught her a lesson, I'm told!

ACTIVITY 24. Write a *new* first sentence for the story in a Readers Theatre script. Follow this with a *new* opening paragraph. Make sure your first sentence is concise, clear, simple, melodic, intriguing, and well-structured. Make sure your paragraph grabs and holds the attention of the audience, sets the theme and mood, and leads swiftly into the action of the story.

ACTIVITY 25. Now that you have some experience with Readers Theatre scripts, choose a folktale, fairy tale, legend, or myth, and turn it into a Readers Theatre script. Assign parts, read, rehearse, and perform for your class.

ACTIVITY 26. After a classroom reading of a Readers Theatre script, ask students to return to their desks and retell the story in written form using their own words. Encourage writers to experiment and create their own unique versions of the tale.

"Recently, while presenting a drama session, I was interviewing a student who decided that she wanted to become the frog who lived in a forest where there was much mischief going on. When I asked her if she were ever put under a spell, she answered in the role of the *frog*: 'I can't really remember. I seem to have lived here for ever and ever. Once upon a time I used to be somebody else'... When the students 'become' someone else and enter the fictional 'here and now,' they have the opportunity to work inside a story connecting their own emotions, experiences, and values with the situations and themes of literature. This is drama. [As teachers] We can provide activities that promote communication skills, creative problem-solving, cooperative interaction, and a sense of the creative arts. This, too, is drama."

DRAMATHEMES. Larry Swartz, Pembroke Publishers, 1988. 528 Hood Road, Markham, ON. Canada L3R 3K9.

SPRINGBOARDS TO CREATIVE DRAMA: NINE DRAMA ACTIVITIES

Activity 1: Putty in my Hands!

Divide your students into pairs. One student is the "sculptor," the other is the "clay." The clay starts in a neutral position, standing or squatting. The sculptor molds the clay into a statue which represents a character, prop, or object from a reader script recently read in class.

Here's the challenge: the clay must be flexible, but also hold any position the sculptor indicates. Sculptors will give special attention to details (facial expression, stance, mood). There should be no talking during this activity until the sculptor has finished a work. Then, magically, a statue may be tapped on the head and given life to move and speak in character. Observers may ask questions and guess identities, if you wish.

Activity 2: *Yesterday's News*

Here's another activity based on the same premise. Divide students into pairs. Again, one student is the "artist," the other is the "mannequin." Using newspaper, scissors, and tape, each artist dresses a mannequin in a newspaper costume which represents a character in a reader script recently read in class.

Again, the mannequin magically comes alive when tapped on the head and begins to move and speak in character. Another tap on the head will *silence* the mannequin while observers guess just which character is being represented.

Activity 3: *Hey, Mom, I'm on TV!*

Divide students into pairs again and ask them to improvise a TV interview with a character in one of your reader scripts. Give each pair a few minutes to plan questions and possible answers, if you wish. If not, ask them to improvise *on the spot*! Each student should have a chance to interview *and* be interviewed.

Activity 4: *The Untold Story*

Divide students into groups and ask them to improvise a scene showing something which happened *right before* or *directly after* the story action in a reader script. These happenings will come from the group's collective imagination and add scope and depth to the reading experience. Who knows? Your groups may come up with viable new reader script stories of their own.

Activity 5: *Draw, Partner! A Drama Game*

Provide large sheets of paper and marker pens for groups of three or four students. Then divide these groups into two or three "teams."

Teacher calls one representative from each group and tells them all a word or phrase which comes from a reader script story read by the entire class. The representatives rush back to their groups to communicate the message by drawing it on a large sheet of paper.

The first team to guess correctly shouts out and wins a point. Continue until all group members have drawn. The team with the most points wins.

Activity 6: Pass the Blob!

Place students in a circle on the floor. One student is selected to "start the blob!" This student silently uses his/her hands to create (from an invisible clay "blob") an object or character from a recently read reader script story. When the creation is finished, the creator passes it carefully on to the next person and announces to all what has been created. The next person reworks the "blob" and creates something new. The action continues until the entire circle has had a chance to "pass the blob!"

Activity 7: Behind the Mask

Ask students to create a mask from easily found materials in the classroom or art room. The masks should represent characters from reader script stories which have been read in the classroom.

Divide mask makers into groups and ask students to hold masks in front of their faces as they create a group tableau of "frozen" figures. On a signal, figures can freeze into different positions, then come to life and move in character until they freeze again.

Teacher may also tap frozen figures at random and ask them questions about their characters which they must answer in character. Repeat until interest wanes.

Activity 8: Script Characters in Outer Space

A character from a reader script is taken from his/her story and transplanted to an alien planet, somewhere in outer space. The aliens question him/her about story life while the character (staying in character) questions the aliens.

Activity 9: Dramatizing Your Readers Theatre Scripts

Try some collaborative dramas by asking a group of students to dramatize any of the Readers Theatre scripts in their own way. (Any mixture of reading levels can be involved in the dramatization.) Participants may assign roles and re-enact the tale either by acting the parts themselves, or portraying part or all of the characters using body puppets, cardboard cutouts, store mannequins, papier-mâché statues, etc. Costume pieces, props, or masks might be used. The sky's the limit and imagination reigns. Remind students that, unlike the Readers Theatre script version, gesture, action, and theatrical staging will be needed to make the dramatization come alive!

31

TWO TAKE PART READ-ALOUD SCRIPTS FOR USE IN THE CLASSROOM

The following two Readers Theatre scripts have been included in this book to help teachers and students get started. Both scripts work well as instant or cooperative readings in the classroom, but are especially successful when rehearsed, polished, and performed! For each script you will find two versions: a Teacher Script complete with staging suggestions, entrance ideas and vocabulary information, and a Reader Script which may be duplicated for each of your readers and/or entire classroom.

The Crazy Critters: This script has been especially designed for older readers to rehearse and then perform for younger readers. It is an especially fun script because it involves the use of costume pieces, quick changes, and hand-held placards which introduce and reinforce some of the special vocabulary words found in the piece. As the reading progresses, all readers get to read and experiment with the part of the "funny old man." A special color-me poster has been included which may be duplicated and passed out to young audience members at the end of the performance.

The Fish Tank: This script is a longer and more challenging script which will need much rehearsing to bring to performance level. It is best read by older students who can rise to the challenge. Student readers will be asked to examine the characters' inner feelings and express these feelings through voice, gesture, facial expression, and posture. Here is a chance to discuss plot, character, point of view, setting, style, and any special narrative techniques. The Teacher Script includes suggested stage set-up and extensive blocking, but you may wish to encourage your readers to create their own.

NOTE: The numerals running vertically down the left margin of each page of dialog are for the convenience of the director. With these, he/she may easily direct attention to a specific passage.

The Crazy Critters

by Lois Walker

A presentation for young audiences

Teacher Script

CAST OF CHARACTERS

TEACHER/NARRATOR

READER 1

READER 2

READER 3

READER 4

READER 5

Arrange one large chair and five small chairs as shown.

ENTRANCES

Teacher/Narrator enters, walks to large chair, faces audience, and says, "This looks like the right chair for me! I think I'll sit down and quietly read a crazy story while I wait."

Reader 1 enters with folder open, pretending to read silently. Reader 1 walks to proper chair, looks up and asks the teacher, "What are you doing Mr./Mrs. _____?" Teacher/Narrator looks up and says, "I'm reading a crazy story while I wait."

Readers 2, 3 and 4 enter with folders open, pretending to read silently. Readers 2, 3 and 4 walk to proper chairs, look up and ask, "What are you doing, teacher?" Teacher/Narrator looks up and says, "We're reading crazy stories while we wait." Readers 2, 3 and 4 answer, "We will too!" They sit in proper chairs and also pretend to read silently.

Reader 5 runs in with folder under arm and screeches to a halt just in front of proper chair. Reader 5 says, "What are you all doing?" Teacher/Narrator and Readers 1, 2, 3 and 4 look up and say in unison, "We're reading *crazy stories* while *we wait*!"

Reader 5 says, "Who are you waiting for?" All answer, *"You!"*

Reader 5 smiles at audience and sits. The reading begins.

VOCABULARY LIST

camel:	noun. a beast of burden with a humped back, found in Asia.
llama:	noun. a camel-like but humpless beast of burden having white or brownish thick woolly hair, found in South America.
chimpanzee:	noun. an African ape having large ears and brown hair.
giraffe:	noun. the tallest of all animals, with a long neck and slender limbs, found in Africa.
kangaroo:	noun. An Australian marsupial with short, weak forelimbs and powerful hind limbs.
dinosaur:	noun. family of extinct reptiles, including the largest-known land animals.
joey:	noun. a young animal, especially a young kangaroo.

Note: The words *surprised, amazed, dumbfounded, bewildered* and *astonished* are featured in this story.

Teacher Script

1
2
3   *(Props or costume pieces may be used as each READER takes role of the*
4   *funny old man. For example: Strange hat, glasses with false nose, and*
5   *walking cane. As reading begins, props and costumes are under*
6   *READER 1's chair. These items will be passed from READER to*
7   *READER as the reading progresses.)*
8   *(Large signs with the following words printed on them will also be*
9   *needed: Surprised, amazed, dumbfounded, bewildered, and*
10 *astonished. Signs may be glued to holding sticks, if desired. These will*
11 *be kept on floor in front of appropriate READERS until called for in the*
12 *script.)*
13 **NARRATOR: Late last Monday**
14   **It happened, you see,**
15 **READER 1: A funny old man** *(READER 1 puts on hat and glasses, takes*
16   *cane.)*
17 **READER 2: Shuffled up to me.**
18 **READER 3: He pointed his finger**
19 **READER 4:   And scratched his head.** *(READER 1 stands and shuffles*
20   *Downstage Center, pretending to be the old man. READER 1 stands*
21   *facing audience.)*
22 **READER 5: Then this is what the old man said,**
23   *(The following word must be said just as it is written: "Ex-cue-ooooz" is*
24   *pronounced as three syllables. "Ooooz" and "me" are emphasized.*
25   *Rehearse this by establishing a beat or rhythm which will be used*
26   *throughout the story when these words appear.)*
27 **ALL: "Ex-cue-ooooz me!**
28   *(READER 1 points cane or wags finger at audience during following*
29   *poem. Note: Depending on class reading level, READER 1 may actually*
30   *read the poem instead of NARRATOR.)*
31 **NARRATOR: Is that your mama**
32   **With the thick woolly hair,**
33   **Looks like a camel**
34   **But her back is bare?**
35
36   **She's lost her hump!**
37   **And I'll tell you, too,**
38   **That crazy critter looks a lot**

1   **ALL:** *(READERS point to audience in unison on "Like you!")* **Like you!"**

2   *(READER 1 returns to chair and passes props and costumes to READER 2.)*

3   **NARRATOR: As you can well imagine,**

4   **I was**

5   **READER 5:** *(Picks up sign which says "Surprised," stands, and holds sign*

6   *above head.)* **Surprised!** *(NARRATOR stands. READER 5 sits and places*

7   *sign on floor.)*

8   **NARRATOR: I began to feel**

9   **Thick woolly hair**

10   **Sprouting on my body**

11   **Everywhere.**

12

13   **"No, no!" I cried.**

14   **"That's not my mama.**

15   **That crazy critter is just a**

16   **ALL:** *Llama."*

17   **NARRATOR:** *(Sits.)* **Late last Tuesday**

18   **It happened, you see,**

19   **READER 1: A funny old man** *(READER 2 puts on hat and glasses, takes*

20   *cane.)*

21   **READER 2: Shuffled up to me.**

22   **READER 3: He pointed his finger**

23   **READER 4:   And scratched his head.** *(READER 2 stands and shuffles*

24   *Downstage Center, pretending to be the old man. READER 2 stands*

25   *facing audience.)*

26   **READER 5: Then this is what the old man said,**

27   **ALL:** *(Same directions as earlier.)***"Ex-cue-ooooz me!**

28   *(READER 2 points cane or wags finger just as READER 1 did earlier.*

29   *Again, READER 2 may read following, if desired:)*

30   **NARRATOR: Is that your papa**

31   **With the black hairy knees**

32   **And short bowed legs,**

33   **Swinging through the trees?**

34

35   **He's up to monkey business.**

36   **And I'll tell you, too,**

37   **That crazy critter looks a lot**

38   **ALL:** *(All READERS point to audience in unison on "Like you!")* **Like you!"**

1   **NARRATOR: As you can well imagine,**

2   **I was**

3   **READER 4:** *(READER 4 stands, holds "Amazed" sign high and reads:)*

4   **Amazed!** *(NARRATOR stands. READER 4 sits and places sign on floor.)*

5   **NARRATOR: I looked right down**

6   **For I wanted to know,**

7   **And my short little legs**

8   **Were beginning to bow.**

9

10   **"No, no!" I cried**

11   **"It's plain to see.**

12   **That crazy critter is a**

13   **ALL:** *Chimpanzee."*

14   **NARRATOR:** *(Sits.)* **Late last Wednesday**

15   **It happened, you see,**

16   **READER 1: A funny old man**

17   *(READER 3 has received props and costume from READER 2 and*

18   *prepares to play the old man.)*

19   **READER 2: Shuffled up to me.**

20   **READER 3: He pointed his finger**

21   **READER 4: And scratched his head.** *(READER 3 shuffles to Downstage*

22   *Center and faces audience.)*

23   **READER 5: Then this is what the old man said,**

24   **ALL:** *(Read as before.)* ***"Ex-cue-ooooz me!***

25   **NARRATOR: Is that your brother**

26   **With his nose held high,**

27   **Spotted feet on the ground,**

28   **Head in the sky?**

29

30   **He's got a long neck!**

31   **And I'll tell you, too,**

32   **That crazy critter looks a lot**

33   **ALL:** *(All READERS point to audience in unison on "Like you!")* **Like you!"**

34   **NARRATOR: As you can well imagine,**

35   **I was**

36   **READER 2:** *(Stands and holds up "Dumbfounded' sign.)* **Dumbfounded.**

37   *(NARRATOR stands. READER 2 sits and places sign on floor.)*

38   **NARRATOR: I felt my neck**

1   And what do you know?

2   The whole darn thing

3   Was beginning to grow!

4

5   "No, no!" I cried.

6   And I tried to laugh.

7   "That crazy critter is a tall

8   **ALL:** *Giraffe."*

9   **NARRATOR:** *(Sits.)* Late last Thursday

10   It happened, you see,

11   **READER 1:** A funny old man *(READER 4 puts on hat and glasses, takes*

12   *cane.)*

13   **READER 2:** Shuffled up to me.

14   **READER 3:** He pointed his finger

15   **READER 4:** And scratched his head. *(READER 4 reads line, then stands*

16   *and shuffles Downstage Center, pretending to be the old man. READER*

17   *4 stands facing audience.)*

18   **READER 5:** Then this is what the old man said,

19   **ALL:** *(Read as before.)* **Ex-cue-ooooz me!** *(READER 4 points as has been*

20   *done before. READER 4 may also read following, if desired.)*

21   **NARRATOR:** Is that your sister

22   With the built-in pouch,

23   Hopping on her hind legs

24   Acting like a grouch?

25   **NARRATOR:** She's got a little joey.

26   And I'll tell you, too,

27   That crazy critter looks a lot

28   **ALL:** *(All READERS point to audience in unison on "Like you!")* **Like you!"**

29   **NARRATOR:** As you can well imagine,

30   I was

31   **READER 3:** *(Stands and holds "Bewildered" sign high.)* **Bewildered.**

32   *(NARRATOR stands. READER 3 sits and places sign on floor.)*

33   **NARRATOR:** I didn't have a sister

34   Who acted like a grouch.

35   But for some strange reason,

36   I *did* have a pouch.

37

38   "No, no!" I cried.

1   "I know what's true.

2   That crazy critter is a

3   **ALL:** *Kangaroo."*

4   **NARRATOR:** *(Sits.)* **Late last Friday**

5   **It happened, you see,**

6   **READER 1: A funny old man** *(READER 5 now plays the funny old man.)*

7   **READER 2: Shuffled up to me.**

8   **READER 3: He pointed his finger**

9   **READER 4: And scratched his head.** *(READER 5 shuffles to Downstage*

10   *spot and does as others have done.)*

11   **READER 5: Then this is what the old man said,**

12   **ALL:** *(Read with enthusiasm.)* **"Ex-cue-ooooz me!**

13   **NARRATOR: Is that your uncle**

14   **With the powerful jaws,**

15   **Giant lizard body,**

16   **And sharp clutching claws?**

17

18   **He's a grand old fossil.**

19   **And I'll tell you, too,**

20   **That crazy critter looks a lot**

21   **ALL:** *(All READERS point to audience.)* **Like you!"**

22   **NARRATOR: As you can well imagine,**

23   **I was**

24   **READER 1:** *(Stands and holds "Astonished" sign high.)* **Astonished.**

25   *(NARRATOR stands. READER 1 sits.)*

26   **NARRATOR: My lizard lips**

27   **Began to pout.**

28   **My lizard tongue**

29   **Flashed in and out.**

30

31   **"No, no!" I cried.**

32   **"Please say no more.**

33   **That crazy critter is a**

34   **ALL:** *Dinosaur."*

35   **NARRATOR:** *(Sits.)* **Late this morning**

36   **I woke in bed,**

37   **Thoughts of critters**

38   **In my head.**

1   **Ran to the mirror**

2   **And what did I see?**

3 **READER 1:** *(Stands.)* ***No* hair from a llama.**

4 **READER 2:** *(Stands.)* ***No* legs from a chimpanzee.**

5 **READER 3:** *(Stands.)* ***No* neck from a giraffe.**

6 **READER 4:** *(Stands.)* ***No* pouch from a kangaroo.**

7 **READER 5:** *(Stands.)* ***No* lips from a dinosaur.**

8 **NARRATOR:** *(Stands.)* **I just saw *me*!**

9   **And I made myself a promise**

10   **Which I plan to keep:**

11 **ALL:** ***No more eating pizza***

12   ***Before I go to sleep!***

13

14

15

16

17

18

19

20

21

22

23

24

25

26

27

28

29

30

31

32

33

34

35

36

37

38

Poster can be duplicated and handed out to members of the audience after the reading is finished.

1   **Reader Script**

2   *(for duplication)*

3

4   **NARRATOR:** Late last Monday

5   It happened, you see,

6   **READER 1:** A funny old man

7   **READER 2:** Shuffled up to me.

8   **READER 3:** He pointed his finger

9   **READER 4:** And scratched his head.

10   **READER 5:** Then this is what the old man said,

11   **ALL:** *"Ex-cue-ooooz me!*

12   **NARRATOR:** Is that your mama

13   With the thick woolly hair,

14   Looks like a camel

15   But her back is bare?

16

17   She's lost her hump!

18   And I'll tell you, too,

19   That crazy critter looks a lot

20   **ALL:** *Like you!"*

21   **NARRATOR:** As you can well imagine,

22   I was

23   **READER 5:** Surprised!

24   **NARRATOR:** I began to feel

25   Thick woolly hair

26   Sprouting on my body

27   Everywhere.

28

29   "No, no!" I cried.

30   "That's not my mama.

31   That crazy critter is just a

32   **ALL:** *Llama."*

33   **NARRATOR:** Late last Tuesday

34   It happened, you see,

35   **READER 1:** A funny old man

36   **READER 2:** Shuffled up to me.

37   **READER 3:** He pointed his finger

38   **READER 4:** And scratched his head.

1 **READER 5:** Then this is what the old man said,

2 **ALL:** *"Ex-cue-ooooz me!*

3 **NARRATOR:** Is that your papa

4   With the black hairy knees

5   And short bowed legs,

6   Swinging through the trees?

7

8   He's up to monkey business.

9   And I'll tell you, too,

10   That crazy critter looks a lot

11 **ALL:** *Like you!"*

12 **NARRATOR:** As you can well imagine,

13   I was

14 **READER 4:** Amazed!

15 **NARRATOR:** I looked right down

16   For I wanted to know,

17   And my short little legs

18   Were beginning to bow.

19

20   "No, no!" I cried

21   "It's plain to see.

22   That crazy critter is a

23 **ALL:** *Chimpanzee."*

24 **NARRATOR:** Late last Wednesday

25   It happened, you see,

26 **READER 1:** A funny old man

27 **READER 2:** Shuffled up to me.

28 **READER 3:** He pointed his finger

29 **READER 4:** And scratched his head.

30 **READER 5:** Then this is what the old man said,

31 **ALL:** *"Ex-cue-ooooz me!*

32 **NARRATOR:** Is that your brother

33   With his nose held high,

34   Spotted feet on the ground,

35   Head in the sky?

36

37   He's got a long neck!

38   And I'll tell you, too,

1   That crazy critter looks a lot
2   ALL: *Like you!"*
3   NARRATOR: As you can well imagine,
4   I was
5   READER 2: Dumbfounded.
6   NARRATOR: I felt my neck
7   And what do you know?
8   The whole darn thing
9   Was beginning to grow!
10
11   "No, no!" I cried.
12   And I tried to laugh.
13   "That crazy critter is a tall
14 ALL: *Giraffe."*
15 NARRATOR: Late last Thursday
16   It happened, you see,
17 READER 1: A funny old man
18 READER 2: Shuffled up to me.
19 READER 3: He pointed his finger
20 READER 4: And scratched his head.
21 READER 5: Then this is what the old man said,
22 ALL: *"Ex-cue-ooooz me!*
23 NARRATOR: Is that your sister
24   With the built-in pouch,
25   Hopping on her hind legs
26   Acting like a grouch?
27
28   She's got a little joey.
29   And I'll tell you, too,
30   That crazy critter looks a lot
31 ALL: *Like you!"*
32 NARRATOR: As you can well imagine,
33   I was
34 READER 3: Bewildered.
35 NARRATOR: I didn't have a sister
36   Who acted like a grouch.
37   But for some strange reason,
38   I did have a pouch.

1   "No, no!" I cried

2   "I know what's true.

3   That crazy critter is a

4   ALL: *Kangaroo."*

5   NARRATOR: Late last Friday

6   It happened, you see,

7   READER 1: A funny old man

8   READER 2: Shuffled up to me.

9   READER 3: He pointed his finger

10 READER 4: And scratched his head.

11 READER 5: Then this is what the old man said,

12 ALL: *Ex-cue-ooooz me!*

13 NARRATOR: Is that your uncle

14   With the powerful jaws,

15   Giant lizard body,

16   And sharp clutching claws?

17

18   He's a grand old fossil.

19   And I'll tell you, too,

20   That crazy critter looks a lot

21 ALL: *Like you!"*

22 NARRATOR: As you can well imagine,

23   I was

24 READER 1: Astonished.

25 NARRATOR: My lizard lips

26   Began to pout.

27   My lizard tongue

28   Flashed in and out.

29 NARRATOR: "No, no!" I cried.

30   "Please say no more.

31   That crazy critter is a

32 ALL: *Dinosaur."*

33 NARRATOR: Late this morning

34   I woke in bed,

35   Thoughts of critters

36   In my head.

37

38   Ran to the mirror

1   And what did I see?
2   READER 1: No hair from a llama.
3   READER 2: No legs from a chimpanzee.
4   READER 3: No neck from a giraffe.
5   READER 4: No pouch from a kangaroo.
6   READER 5: No lips from a dinosaur.
7   NARRATOR: I just saw me!
8   And I made myself a promise
9   Which I plan to keep:
10   ALL: *No more eating pizza*
11   *Before I go to sleep!*
12
13
14
15
16
17
18
19
20
21
22
23
24
25
26
27
28
29
30
31
32
33
34
35
36
37
38

The Fish Tank

by Lee Karvonen

Intermediate readers

Teacher Script

CAST OF CHARACTERS

NARRATOR 1

NARRATOR 2

FATHER

MOTHER

BROTHER

SISTER

MATTHEW or MICHELE

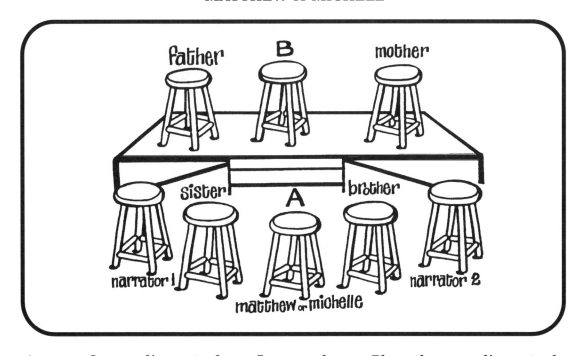

Arrange five medium stools on floor, as shown. Place three medium stools on slightly elevated platform behind and above stools on floor. Place six adjustable music stands in front of Narrators 1 and 2, Father, Mother, Sister and Brother. Matthew or Michele will hold script in hands to allow for freer movement. All readers are sitting as the reading begins.

ENTRANCES

A simple entrance works best for this script. Ask Mother, Father, Sister, and Brother to enter from anywhere in the room. Each carries folder in same (right or left) arm and walks directly to assigned stool. Readers sit, place folders on music stands, and open folders to page 1.

Next, Narrators 1 and 2 enter carrying folders in same arms and walk to their assigned stools. Narrators sit, place folders on music stands, and open folders to page 1.

Matthew (or Michele — with a few minor line changes, a girl can take this role as well as a boy) walks to stool "A" carrying folder. He/she opens folder, looks up, smiles at audience, and introduces him/herself. "I'm Jamie Walker and I will read the role of Matthew." In turn, all readers introduce themselves this way. When all have been introduced, the reading begins.

VOCABULARY LIST

aquarium: noun. an exhibition tank for aquatic animals or plants.

reflect: verb. mirroring or giving back an image.

transform: verb. to give a different form or appearance to.

porpoise: noun. a five- to six-foot dolphin-like mammal with a blunt, rounded snout.

shepherd: noun. a keeper or herder of sheep.

timpani: noun. plural. kettle drums.

1 **Teacher Script**

2

3 **NARRATOR 1: Matthew lived in a noisy house.**

4 **NARRATOR 2: His father always yelled when he spoke to anyone.**

5 **FATHER:** *(Stands.)* **"A noisy house is a busy house!"**

6 **NARRATOR 1: His mother always seemed to be nagging him loudly.**

7 **MOTHER:** *(Stands.)* **"Matthew! Have you cleaned up that junk pile you**
8 **call your room?"**

9 **NARRATOR 2: His brother played his CDs so loudly that the wall**
10 **between their rooms would shake.**

11 **NARRATOR 1: And sometimes his brother would sort of yell along.**

12 **BROTHER:** *(Stands.)* **"Ooh, Baby! Ooh, Baby! Ooh, Baby! Ooh!"**
13 *(MOTHER, FATHER and BROTHER sit.)*

14 **NARRATOR 2: Matthew didn't like all the noise. Often, he retreated to**
15 **the quiet of his bedroom and spent hours staring at his aquarium.**
16 **The aquarium stood on a nightstand right beside his pillow and was**
17 **filled with beautiful, multicolored tropical fish.**

18 **MATTHEW: "You fish are so lucky. You get to live in a quiet, peaceful**
19 **world. As long as I feed you, you have no worries at all."**

20 **NARRATOR 1: Sometimes his sister burst into his room.**

21 **SISTER:** *(Stands.)* **"Matthew! Why don't you let those poor fish go?"**

22 **NARRATOR 2: His sister had taken an environmental unit in school and**
23 **now wanted to free every animal in the world, including the**
24 **neighbor's dog.**

25 **SISTER: "Are you as stupid as those poor fish or are you going to answer**
26 **me?"**

27 **MATTHEW: "They like it in the tank. It's safe for them."**

28 **SISTER: "How would you like to live in a tank, Matthew?"**

29 **NARRATOR 1: Matthew smiled and thought about that.**

30 **MATTHEW: "I think I'd like it. It would be so peaceful and quiet."**

31 **SISTER:** *(Yells.)* **"You're impossible!"**

32 **NARRATOR 2: Matthew's sister slammed the door as hard as she could.**
33 *(SISTER stomps on floor and sits.)*

34 **NARRATOR 1: Downstairs Matthew's parents were becoming tired of**
35 **all the yelling, door slamming, and music blaring, so they yelled up.**

36 **FATHER:** *(Stands.)* **"That'll be enough of that kind of noise! How about**
37 **a bit of busy noise?"**

38 **MOTHER:** *(Stands.)* **"Matthew! Have you cleaned your room yet?"**

1   NARRATOR 2: Upstairs Matthew's brother opened his bedroom door
2   and called out,
3   BROTHER: "No, Mom! He's too busy watching his little fishies!"
4   NARRATOR 1: Matthew opened his bedroom door too, but he didn't
5   speak, he just listened.
6   FATHER: "I don't know what's wrong with the boy! He just does not
7   have any ambition!"
8   MOTHER: "Please, George, lower your voice. He'll hear you!"
9   FATHER: "Oh, no, he won't! He'll be too busy staring at those fish to
10   hear a word we say. Why can't he be like a normal boy and play
11   hockey or football or even ride a bike? Now that's normal!"
12 MOTHER: "I know, George, but we can't force him."
13 FATHER: "Maybe we can! Maybe, without his precious fish, we'd get a
14   little cooperation out of him!" *(FATHER and MOTHER sit.)*
15 NARRATOR 2: Upstairs Matthew felt a chill run through his body. He
16   ran across the room and hugged the tank, pressing his cheek
17   against the cool glass.
18 MATTHEW: *(Stands.)* "No! Please, no! Not my fish!" *(MATTHEW sits, sadly*
19   *and slowly.)*
20 NARRATOR 1: Matthew gazed at his beautiful fish, gliding carefree
21   among the rocks, reeds, and tiny castle in the tank. *(MATTHEW*
22   *gazes straight ahead as though looking at tank.)*
23 MATTHEW: "You fish are so lucky! I wish I could be just like you. No
24   worries. No family. Just peace and quiet, always."
25 NARRATOR 2: Matthew hugged the tank even harder and just watched
26   his fish. An hour passed, *(MATTHEW nods head, then turns around*
27   *slowly and sits with back to audience.)*
28 NARRATOR 1: and Matthew finally began to relax. Gradually he drifted
29   off to sleep.
30 NARRATOR 2: *(Stands.)* Downstairs the rest of the family gathered to
31   watch TV in the family room.
32 NARRATOR 1: *(Stands suddenly.)* Suddenly, outside, the sky split open
33   with a giant fork of lightning.
34 NARRATOR 2: The lights flickered and then the house seemed to
35   tremble with the following explosion of thunder. *(All READERS*
36   *stomp their feet once on the floor, making thunder crash. NARRATORS*
37   *1 and 2 sit. SISTER stands.)*
38 SISTER: "This storm is going to ruin my favorite program! I'm going to

The Fish Tank

1   bed!"

2   **BROTHER:** *(Stands.)* **"Scared of a little thunder, aren't ya? Gonna hide?"**

3   **FATHER:** *(Stands and stretches. MOTHER stands too.)* **"That'll be enough**
4   **of that! I think it's time we all went to bed!"**

5   **MOTHER:** **"Yes, remember, school tomorrow."**

6   **BRO/SIS:** **"Mom! Don't remind us!"** *(All sit.)*

7   **NARRATOR 1: The house was soon dark, except for the glow from the**
8   **tank light. Matthew slept deeply, through the noise of the storm.**
9   *(MATTHEW moves to stool "B" on the platform. He sits facing audience.)*

10   **NARRATOR 2:** *(Stands.)* **Suddenly lightning flared in the room and**
11   **Matthew woke with a start.** *(MATTHEW jumps to his feet and mimes*
12   *the action from in front of stool "B.")*

13   **NARRATOR 1:** *(Stands.)* **He looked at his reflection in the side of the**
14   **tank and could not believe his eyes.**

15   **NARRATOR 2: His wish had been granted. He had been transformed.**
16   **He was a fish!**

17   **MATTHEW:** *(Looks at audience and announces:)* **"I'm a fish! Wow! I'm**
18   **really a fish! This is awesome!"** *(MATTHEW bends, waves, whirls,*
19   *miming the swim.)*

20   **NARRATOR 1: Happily, Matthew dove deep into the fish tank, heading**
21   **toward the tiny castle. Then he turned pure porpoise, exploring**
22   **every corner of his watery paradise at full speed.**

23   **NARRATOR 2: And for the next while, Matthew had the time of his life,**
24   **diving, swirling, and racing past the other fish in his fish tank.**

25   **NARRATOR 1: Suddenly, Matthew felt his stomach growl. A flash of**
26   **lightning revealed his bedside clock. It was time to feed his fish.**
27   *(MATTHEW rubs stomach.)*

28   **MATTHEW: "Wait a minute! How can I feed the fish? I *am* a fish!"**

29   **NARRATOR 2: Matthew was the only person in the family who ever fed**
30   **the fish. He was in trouble.** *(MATTHEW slowly sits as this information*
31   *sinks in.)*

32   **NARRATOR 1: As the night crept on and the storm slowly ebbed,**
33   **Matthew began to have second thoughts about being a fish.**

34   **MATTHEW: "I could starve to death! My fish and I are in trouble!"**
35   *(MATTHEW turns around slowly and sits on stool "B" with back to*
36   *audience.)*

37   **NARRATOR 2: Soon morning arrived. Mother was downstairs and**
38   **breakfast was almost ready.**

1 MOTHER: *(Stands.)* "George! Children! Come and get it!"

2 FATHER: *(Stands.)* "You don't have to call me twice! I could eat a horse!"

3 SISTER: *(Stands.)* "Dad! That's so gross! We shouldn't eat animals!"

4 BROTHER: *(Stands.)* "Are we having horse for breakfast? I was hoping
5   for a little *fried fish*!"

6 MOTHER: "That's not funny! Now call your brother. He loves pancakes."

7 NARRATOR 1: Matthew's brother leaned into the hall and yelled up to
8   Matthew.

9 BROTHER: *(Leans and yells.)* "Hey, fish lips! Breakfast!"

10 NARRATOR 2: There was no answer. *(All sit except MOTHER. NARRATOR
11   1 stands.)*

12 NARRATOR 1: Matthew's mother went up to his room. *(MOTHER walks
13   forward and looks down at the empty stool "A." NARRATOR 2 stands.)*

14 NARRATOR 2: She saw the unmade bed. A frown spread across her face.
15   *(MOTHER looks worried.)*

16 MOTHER: "Matthew? Matthew, where are you? Matthew!"

17 NARRATOR 1: Now she was worried. She looked in his closet. She
18   rushed to the bathroom.

19 MOTHER: *(Turns to her left.)* "Matthew? Please answer me! Matthew?"
20   *(FATHER jumps up, then BROTHER and SISTER jump up.)*

21 NARRATOR 2: Everybody ran up to Matthew's room. *(FATHER, MOTHER,
22   BROTHER and SISTER are all standing, looking at empty stool "A.")*
23   They all looked worried. Matthew watched, not really able to believe
24   that his family was so concerned.

25 MATTHEW: *(Turns on stool "B" and faces audience.)* "I didn't think they
26   cared if I was around or not. They all seemed to hate me and
27   everything I did."

28 NARRATOR 1: Matthew wished he could tell them where he was, that
29   he was all right.

30 NARRATOR 2: Then his father suddenly left the room. *(FATHER turns
31   his back to audience.)*

32 NARRATOR 1: He was back in a few minutes, his head hanging.

33 FATHER: *(Faces front again.)* "I phoned the police and the hospital. No
34   one answering Matthew's description is there." *(FATHER sits and
35   puts head in hands. The rest of the family sits, heads in hands.)*

36 NARRATOR 2: He slumped onto the bed, his head in his hands.

37 SISTER: "Mom? Do you think Matthew ran away?"

38 MOTHER: "He'll be back. I know he'll be back."

1   **FATHER: "Maybe it was me! Maybe I drove him away! I was awfully hard**
2   **on him!"** *(MATTHEW stands and mimes waving back and forth.)*

3   **NARRATOR 1: Matthew swirled around the tank, trying to get their**
4   **attention, but they didn't look toward the tank. Even if they had,**
5   **none of them would have known the silvery fish pressed to the glass**
6   **was Matthew.**

7   **NARRATOR 2: Finally, they left and the day dragged on.** *(Family*
8   *members seated on stools turn their backs to audience.)*

9   **NARRATOR 1: Later that night, Matthew's family lay in their beds,**
10   **restless and unable to sleep. Each one thought about Matthew.**

11   **FATHER:** *(Turns and faces audience.)* **"I know he ran away. It's all my**
12   **fault."**

13   **MOTHER:** *(Turns and faces audience.)* **"I hope he's warm enough and**
14   **has something to eat."**

15   **BROTHER:** *(Faces audience.)* **"He's not such a bad kid. I wish I hadn't**
16   **been so mean."**

17   **SISTER:** *(Faces audience.)* **"He really did look after those fish. I guess he**
18   **really cares about animals too."**

19   **NARRATOR 2: Matthew swam faster and faster in the fish tank. He tried**
20   **to think.** *(MATTHEW turns on the spot.)*

21   **MATTHEW: "How did I get into this mess? How do I get out of it? I don't**
22   **want to be a fish anymore."**

23   **NARRATOR 1: At that moment the sky was again shattered by a fierce**
24   **electrical storm.**

25   **NARRATOR 2: The lightning turned the night into day each time it**
26   **ignited.**

27   **NARRATOR 1: While lightning ripped the sky, the timpani of thunder**
28   **rattled the glass and shuddered the very air.** *(All READERS stomp*
29   *their feet over and over to make thunder sounds. These sound effects*
30   *continue through the next speech.)*

31   **NARRATOR 2: Inside the tank, the fish seemed suspended, awestruck,**
32   **while the enraged elements assaulted the town.**

33   **NARRATOR 1: Matthew blinked, feeling the coolness of the tank against**
34   **his cheek.** *(MATTHEW stretches and yawns, then stares at tank.)*

35   **NARRATOR 2: He stretched and yawned, then stared at the tank.**

36   **NARRATOR 1: His hands flew to his face, stomach, and legs.** *(MATTHEW*
37   *jumps to feet.)*

38   **NARRATOR 2: He ran to the window, yanked it open, and filled his**

1   lungs with rain-sweetened air. *(MATTHEW takes deep breath.)* **He**

2   **yelled,**

3   **MATTHEW: "I'm back! I'm Matthew! I'm really Matthew!"**

4   **NARRATOR 1: His father burst through the door, followed almost**

5   **immediately by everyone else.** *(FATHER stands, then others stand.)*

6   **NARRATOR 2: His father grabbed Matthew and squeezed him so hard**

7   **he nearly cried.**

8   **NARRATOR 1: His mother's arms were around his neck a moment later.**

9   **NARRATOR 2: Soon he felt the arms of his brother and sister.**

10   **NARRATOR 1: Then everybody began to talk at once.**

11   **BROTHER: "Where were you?"**

12   **SISTER: "What happened?"**

13   **MOTHER: "We were worried sick!"**

14   **FATHER: "Matthew, we've been scared to death. Where have you been?**

15   **NARRATOR 2: Matthew knew he could never tell them the truth.**

16   **They'd never believe it. He wasn't even sure he believed what had**

17   **happened.**

18   **FATHER: "Matthew? Matthew, please tell us what happened?"**

19   **MATTHEW: "I ran away. I thought nobody would miss me. I didn't think**

20   **anyone cared."**

21   **FATHER: "Nobody miss you? That's crazy, son. You're a big part of this**

22   **family."**

23   **NARRATOR 1: This was music to Matthew's ears.**

24   **MATTHEW: "I'm sorry I got you all so worried. I just didn't think**

25   **anybody really cared."**

26   **FATHER: "I hope you know now that we care for you very much."**

27   **NARRATOR 2: Then Matthew and his family sat and talked together for**

28   **a long long time.**

29   **NARRATOR 1: Finally, Mother kissed Matthew's forehead and**

30   **shepherded the others out of his room.** *(MOTHER throws kiss in*

31   *MATTHEW's direction, then FATHER, MOTHER, BROTHER and*

32   *SISTER sit.)*

33   **NARRATOR 2: As the door closed behind them, Matthew walked over to**

34   **the tank** *(MATTHEW crouches and looks in direction of audience as*

35   *though he were looking at the fish tank)* **and crouched beside it.**

36   **MATTHEW: "Well, guys. Time to eat. Is everybody ready?"**

37   **NARRATOR 1: He gently shook an extra portion of food onto the water**

38   **and dozens of tiny lips broke the surface, scrambling for the very**

1   late meal. *(MATTHEW mimes the above.)*
2   MATTHEW: "Fill your faces, guys. That's what I'm gonna do. I hope
3   Mom filled the fridge. *(MATTHEW sits, looks at audience, and says:)*
4   And I'm sure glad to be home, even though it *is* a noisy house!"
5
6
7
8
9
10
11
12
13
14
15
16
17
18
19
20
21
22
23
24
25
26
27
28
29
30
31
32
33
34
35
36
37
38

1   **Reader Script**

2   *(for duplication)*

3

4   **NARRATOR 1:** Matthew lived in a noisy house.

5   **NARRATOR 2:** His father always yelled when he spoke to anyone.

6   **FATHER:** "A noisy house is a busy house!"

7   **NARRATOR 1:** His mother always seemed to be nagging him loudly.

8   **MOTHER:** "Matthew! Have you cleaned up that junk pile you call your
9   room?"

10   **NARRATOR 2:** His brother played his CDs so loudly that the wall
11   between their rooms would shake.

12   **NARRATOR 1:** And sometimes his brother would sort of yell along.

13   **BROTHER:** "Ooh, Baby! Ooh, Baby! Ooh, Baby! Ooh!"

14   **NARRATOR 2:** Matthew didn't like all the noise. Often, he retreated to
15   the quiet of his bedroom and spent hours staring at his aquarium.
16   The aquarium stood on a nightstand right beside his pillow and was
17   filled with beautiful, multicolored tropical fish.

18   **MATTHEW:** "You fish are so lucky. You get to live in a quiet, peaceful
19   world. As long as I feed you, you have no worries at all."

20   **NARRATOR 1:** Sometimes his sister burst into his room.

21   **SISTER:** "Matthew! Why don't you let those poor fish go?"

22   **NARRATOR 2:** His sister had taken an environmental unit in school and
23   now wanted to free every animal in the world, including the
24   neighbor's dog.

25   **SISTER:** "Are you as stupid as those poor fish or are you going to answer
26   me?"

27   **MATTHEW:** "They like it in the tank. It's safe for them."

28   **SISTER:** "How would you like to live in a tank, Matthew?"

29   **NARRATOR 1:** Matthew smiled and thought about that.

30   **MATTHEW:** "I think I'd like it. It would be so peaceful and quiet."

31   **SISTER:** "You're impossible!"

32   **NARRATOR 2:** Matthew's sister slammed the door as hard as she could.

33   **NARRATOR 1:** Downstairs Matthew's parents were becoming tired of
34   all the yelling, door slamming, and music blaring, so they yelled up.

35   **FATHER:** "That'll be enough of that kind of noise! How about a bit of
36   busy noise?"

37   **MOTHER:** "Matthew! Have you cleaned your room yet?"

38   **NARRATOR 2:** Upstairs Matthew's brother opened his bedroom door

1   and called out,

2   BROTHER: "No, mom! He's too busy watching his little fishies!"

3   NARRATOR 1: Matthew opened his bedroom door too, but he didn't

4   speak, he just listened.

5   FATHER: "I don't know what's wrong with the boy! He just does not

6   have any ambition!"

7   MOTHER: "Please, George, lower your voice. He'll hear you!"

8   FATHER: "Oh, no, he won't! He'll be too busy staring at those fish to

9   hear a word we say. Why can't he be like a normal boy and play

10   hockey or football or even ride a bike? Now that's normal!"

11   MOTHER: "I know, George, but we can't force him."

12   FATHER: "Maybe we can! Maybe, without his precious fish, we'd get a

13   little cooperation out of him!"

14   NARRATOR 2: Upstairs Matthew felt a chill run through his body. He

15   ran across the room and hugged the tank, pressing his cheek

16   against the cool glass.

17   MATTHEW: "No! Please, no! Not my fish!"

18   NARRATOR 1: Matthew gazed at his beautiful fish, gliding carefree

19   among the rocks, reeds, and tiny castle in the tank.

20   MATTHEW: "You fish are so lucky! I wish I could be just like you. No

21   worries. No family. Just peace and quiet, always."

22   NARRATOR 2: Matthew hugged the tank even harder and just watched

23   his fish. An hour passed,

24   NARRATOR 1: and Matthew finally began to relax. Gradually he drifted

25   off to sleep.

26   NARRATOR 2: Downstairs the rest of the family gathered to watch TV

27   in the family room.

28   NARRATOR 1: Suddenly, outside, the sky split open with a giant fork of

29   lightning.

30   NARRATOR 2: The lights flickered and then the house seemed to

31   tremble with the following explosion of thunder.

32   SISTER: "This storm is going to ruin my favorite program! I'm going to

33   bed!"

34   BROTHER: "Scared of a little thunder, aren't ya? Gonna hide?"

35   FATHER: "That'll be enough of that! I think it's time we all went to bed!"

36   MOTHER: "Yes, remember, school tomorrow."

37   BRO/SIS: "Mom! Don't remind us!"

38   NARRATOR 1: The house was soon dark, except for the glow from the

1   tank light. Matthew slept deeply, through the noise of the storm.

2   NARRATOR 2: Suddenly lightning flared in the room and Matthew

3   woke with a start.

4   NARRATOR 1: He looked at his reflection in the side of the tank and

5   could not believe his eyes.

6   NARRATOR 2: His wish had been granted. He had been transformed.

7   He was a fish!

8   MATTHEW: "I'm a fish! Wow! I'm really a fish! This is awesome!"

9   NARRATOR 1: Happily, Matthew dove deep into the fish tank, heading

10   toward the tiny castle. Then he turned pure porpoise, exploring

11   every corner of his watery paradise at full speed.

12   NARRATOR 2: And for the next while, Matthew had the time of his life,

13   diving, swirling, and racing past the other fish in his fish tank.

14   NARRATOR 1: Suddenly, Matthew felt his stomach growl. A flash of

15   lightning revealed his bedside clock. It was time to feed his fish.

16   MATTHEW: "Wait a minute! How can I feed the fish? I *am* a fish!"

17   NARRATOR 2: Matthew was the only person in the family who ever fed

18   the fish. He was in trouble.

19   NARRATOR 1: As the night crept on and the storm slowly ebbed,

20   Matthew began to have second thoughts about being a fish.

21   MATTHEW: "I could starve to death! My fish and I are in trouble!"

22   NARRATOR 2: Soon morning arrived. Mother was downstairs and

23   breakfast was almost ready.

24   MOTHER: "George! Children! Come and get it!"

25   FATHER: "You don't have to call me twice! I could eat a horse!"

26   SISTER: "Dad! That's so gross! We shouldn't eat animals!"

27   BROTHER: "Are we having horse for breakfast? I was hoping for a little

28   *fried fish*!"

29   MOTHER: "That's not funny! Now call your brother. He loves pancakes."

30   NARRATOR 1: Matthew's brother leaned into the hall and yelled up to

31   Matthew.

32   BROTHER: "Hey, fish lips! Breakfast!"

33   NARRATOR 2: There was no answer.

34   NARRATOR 1: Matthew's mother went up to his room.

35   NARRATOR 2: She saw the unmade bed. A frown spread across her face.

36   MOTHER: "Matthew? Matthew, where are you? Matthew!"

37   NARRATOR 1: Now she was worried. She looked in his closet. She

38   rushed to the bathroom.

1   MOTHER: "Matthew? Please answer me! Matthew?"

2   NARRATOR 2: Everybody ran up to Matthew's room. They all looked

3   worried. Matthew watched, not really able to believe that his family

4   was so concerned.

5   MATTHEW: "I didn't think they cared if I was around or not. They all

6   seemed to hate me and everything I did."

7   NARRATOR 1: Matthew wished he could tell them where he was, that

8   he was all right.

9   NARRATOR 2: Then his father suddenly left the room.

10   NARRATOR 1: He was back in a few minutes, his head hanging.

11   FATHER: "I phoned the police and the hospital. No one answering

12   Matthew's description is there."

13   NARRATOR 2: He slumped onto the bed, his head in his hands.

14   SISTER: "Mom? Do you think Matthew ran away?"

15   MOTHER: "He'll be back. I know he'll be back."

16   FATHER:"Maybe it was me! Maybe I drove him away! I was awfully hard

17   on him!"

18   NARRATOR 1: Matthew swirled around the tank, trying to get their

19   attention, but they didn't look toward the tank. Even if they had,

20   none of them would have known the silvery fish pressed to the glass

21   was Matthew.

22   NARRATOR 2: Finally they left and the day dragged on.

23   NARRATOR 1:   Later that night, Matthew's family lay in their beds,

24   restless and unable to sleep. Each one thought about Matthew.

25   FATHER: "I know he ran away. It's all my fault."

26   MOTHER: "I hope he's warm enough and has something to eat."

27   BROTHER: "He's not such a bad kid. I wish I hadn't been so mean."

28   SISTER: "He really did look after those fish. I guess he really cares about

29   animals too."

30   NARRATOR 2: Matthew swam faster and faster in the fish tank. He tried

31   to think.

32   MATTHEW: "How did I get into this mess? How do I get out of it? I don't

33   want to be a fish anymore."

34   NARRATOR 1: At that moment the sky was again shattered by a fierce

35   electrical storm.

36   NARRATOR 2: The lightning turned the night into day each time it

37   ignited.

38   NARRATOR 1: While lightning ripped the sky, the timpani of thunder

1   rattled the glass and shuddered the very air.

2   NARRATOR 2: Inside the tank, the fish seemed suspended, awestruck,

3   while the enraged elements assaulted the town.

4   NARRATOR 1: Matthew blinked, feeling the coolness of the tank against

5   his cheek.

6   NARRATOR 2: He stretched and yawned, then stared at the tank.

7   NARRATOR 1: His hands flew to his face, stomach, and legs.

8   NARRATOR 2: He ran to the window, yanked it open, and filled his

9   lungs with rain-sweetened air. He yelled,

10   MATTHEW: "I'm back! I'm Matthew! I'm really Matthew!"

11   NARRATOR 1: His father burst through the door, followed almost

12   immediately by everyone else.

13   NARRATOR 2: His father grabbed Matthew and squeezed him so hard

14   he nearly cried.

15   NARRATOR 1: His mother's arms were around his neck a moment later.

16   NARRATOR 2: Soon he felt the arms of his brother and sister.

17   NARRATOR 1: Then everybody began to talk at once.

18   BROTHER: "Where were you?"

19   SISTER: "What happened?"

20   MOTHER: "We were worried sick!"

21   FATHER: "Matthew, we've been scared to death. Where have you been?

22   NARRATOR 2: Matthew knew he could never tell them the truth. They'd

23   never believe it. He wasn't even sure he believed what had

24   happened.

25   FATHER: "Matthew? Matthew, please tell us what happened?"

26   MATTHEW: "I ran away. I thought nobody would miss me. I didn't think

27   anyone cared."

28   FATHER: "Nobody miss you? That's crazy, son. You're a big part of this

29   family."

30   NARRATOR 1: This was music to Matthew's ears.

31   MATTHEW: "I'm sorry I got you all so worried. I just didn't think

32   anybody really cared."

33   FATHER: "I hope you know now that we care for you very much."

34   NARRATOR 2: Then Matthew and his family sat and talked together for

35   a long, long time.

36   NARRATOR 1: Finally, Mother kissed Matthew's forehead and

37   shepherded the others out of his room.

38   NARRATOR 2: As the door closed behind them, Matthew walked over to

1   the tank ... and crouched beside it.

2   MATTHEW: "Well, guys. Time to eat. Is everybody ready?"

3   NARRATOR 1: He gently shook an extra portion of food onto the water

4   and dozens of tiny lips broke the surface, scrambling for the very

5   late meal.

6   MATTHEW: "Fill your faces, guys. That's what I'm gonna do. I hope

7   Mom filled the fridge. And I'm sure glad to be home, even though it

8   *is* a noisy house!"

9

10

11

12

13

14

15

16

17

18

19

20

21

22

23

24

25

26

27

28

29

30

31

32

33

34

35

36

37

38

SOURCES

Adams, Dr. William. "Holiday Harvest," Readers Theatre Script Service, San Diego, CA.

Bauer, Dr. Caroline Feller. *Presenting Reader's Theatre*, H.W. Wilson, Chicago, IL, 1986.

Breen, Robert S. *Chamber Theatre*, Englewood Cliffs, NJ, Prentice-Hall Inc., 1978.

Coger, Leslie Irene & Melvin White. *Readers Theatre Handbook: A Dramatic Approach to Literature.* Third ed. Glenview, IL, Scott Foresman, 1982.

Griffin, Barbara Budge. *Students as Storytellers*, from her "Guidebook Storyteller Series," 10 South Keeneway Drive, Medford, OR, 1989.

McClay, Joanna Hawkins. *Readers Theatre: Toward a Grammar of Practice*, New York, Random House, Inc., 1971.

Readers Theatre News, PO Box 15847, San Diego, CA.

Robertson, M.E. & B. Poston-Anderson. *Readers Theatre: A Practical Guide.* Sydney: Hodder & Stoughton, 1986.

Sealey, Leonard, Nancy Sealey & Marcia Millamore. "Children's Writing," International Reading Association, Newark, DE, 1979.

Swanson, Charlene C. "Reading and Writing Readers Theatre Scripts," Australian Reading Association, *Reading Around: Series Number One,* PO Box 588, WAGGA WAGGA, NSW, March 1988.

Swartz, Larry. *Dramathemes.* Pembroke Publishers, 528 Hood Road, Markham, ON, Canada, 1988.

Walker, Herb & Lois. "Take Part Read-Aloud Story Scripts for Children," Take Part Productions Ltd. West Vancouver, BC, Canada. Publishing since 1988.

White, Mel. *Mel White's Readers Theatre Anthology*, Meriwether Publishing Ltd., Colorado Springs, CO, 1993.

ABOUT THE AUTHOR

Lois Walker (BA, MA) is a former head of the Theatre Department at Notre Dame University, Nelson, B.C. Canada. She is the author of several teachers' resource books, including *The Instant Puppet Resourcebook for Teachers* and *Readers Theatre in the Elementary Classroom*. Through her company, Take Part Productions Ltd., she has created and hosted four award-winning, internationally syndicated television series featuring creative activities for parents, teachers, and children. Her programs are currently seen daily across Canada on YTV, Canada's national youth cable channel. Take Part Productions Ltd. is Canada's largest supplier of Readers Theatre scripts to the educational market.

Readers Theatre Online Canada Website
http://www.fore-tech.com/loiswalker/

Email Lois Walker at lowalker@direct.ca